GREEN ACRE

Poems
By

Cody Shrum

Green Acre ii

Dedication

For Kylee, my first reader and best friend.

Reading Cody Shrum's beautiful debut *Green Acre*, I feel the ache of familiarity, as if the nostalgia he's writing is mine and not his. Even though I can't relate to the specifics (of fishing, of loving Batman), the "shine-wrapped" feeling he's describing belongs to all of us. These poems are about awe, about how the simplest moments of our lives are the most important—sharing stories with family in the car or on the boat, that first kiss with a future spouse "for no reason" (which he knows is actually the best reason). Most people don't realize until much later how important these quiet moments, these "bright whispers" are, but what makes Shrum's work so extraordinary is that he understands their reverence as he lives them.

Melissa Fite Johnson,
author of *Midlife Abecedarian* and *Green*

In Cody Shrum's *Green Acre*, each poem is a world, a story—fishing, driving, a cracked baseball glove, all the luminescence of childhood. Reading made me wistful for my own Kansas childhood. This is a collection of home, and Shrum is a poet who spent time in contemplation of the "life of the river and trees." *Green Acre* paints Midwest constellations reflected in lake water, hummingbirds, I-70, and "useless dinosaur-scaled gar." But underneath the moonlight and nostalgia is an examination of gender: "Dad says dudes don't sing in the car / with other dudes." Over and over, the poet examines his place in the world inside a male body. Tenderness runs through these pages like an undercurrent. Shrum knows how to "dim lanterns to lessen the swarm," and you will leave this collection "golden like waking / from a good, good dream."

Allison Blevins,
author of *Where Will We Live If the House Burns Down?* and *Cataloguing Pain*

I'll begin by using a verb I very rarely use when discussing a book of poetry: I loved reading *Green Acre*. It is not a thrown-together collection of over-the-seasons written or random published poems, but an organized, thematic selection with a beginning, middle and end that I think Aristotle would have admired. There is not an inappropriate word, image, piece of figurative language or dialogue, line or poem in the manuscript and the narrative build and thrust are beautiful. The language is splendid, not a jot or tittle of deliberate incoherence or Institutional Modern Englitsch. I sat down to read a poem or three and then plan a reading schedule. An hour or so later, I finished the manuscript and sat in my reading chair almost transfixed by the experience. On a scale of 1-10 I give Green Acre a rating of 13, my favorite number. It has been a long, long time since I read a manuscript that hit me as delightfully.

David Lee, Apprentice World Class Piddler and
author of *Rusty Barbed Wire*

I read these poems in the passenger seat of a cross country road trip with childhood best friends, an experience unlikely to be replicated, though one I recommend. Shrum's poems wrestle with childhood and home, spotlighting firsts and lasts and struggles and joys and all the in-betweens, in ways that feel like a perfect road trip partner for a drive through your life, be it literal or metaphor.

Aaron Burch,
author of *Year of the Buffalo*
and *A Kind of In-Between*

Contents

First Date at Dr. Plumm's 1
The Day after I Got My First Air Rifle 2
Fishing Stories 3
Big Fish Territory 4
The Death of Santa 5
Mending Time 7
The First Dog I Ever Knew 8
I-70 to St. Louis 9
Dam 10
Catfishing the Elk City Reservoir, ft. Bugs 11
Pests 12
50 Words for Nostalgia 13
So Many Towns Away 14
Chrysalism in November 16
6'4" 300 lb Male Walks Home at Night 17
Catching a 65-Pound Blue Catfish 19
Certainty 22
Nowhere Sunday 23
Back Home 24
The Sound of Casting a Fishing Pole 26
Chiropractic 27
Losing Batman 28
The Losses of Maxine Johnson 30
Counting Hawks 32
An Apologia for This Pint of Boulevard
      Unfiltered Wheat 33
Storm, a Pantoum 34
Sweat and Marijuana 35
Fishing in Illinois by Uncle Rodge's Cabin 37

About the Poet 39
Credits 40
Acknowledgements 41

.

First Date at Dr. Plumm's

After Arne Besser's "Bridgehampton"

The ice cream parlor in my hometown
burnt in a fire that ate a whole city
block, but I can still see it—the beige brick,
red tin awning, doors that squeaked open—
and still taste the rocky road and caramel syrup.

The sky is overcast in autumn
and the wind reaches through buildings
on our small-town main street.
On a seventh-grade Saturday,
the sharp neon tells me:
Homemade Ice Cream and Soda.
She sits across from me and smiles
for the weekend. A bell sounds as
a woman walks out into the cloudy day.

Our mothers dropped us off out front
and mine gave me a ten-dollar bill.
"I'll be back in an hour," she said,
pulling away, eyeing us in her rear view.

So for an hour, we sit and eat ice cream,
talking about seventh-grade things:
which teacher is nicest,
whose lockers stand beside ours.
Smiling, nervous, living in the spaces
before the orange glow of fire
would rip it all apart.

The Day after I Got My First Air Rifle

I killed a cottontail with it.
The sun shone blood orange
in the west, high above
our congregation of bicycles.

You do it! No, you do it!
I dare you! I did it. I
pumped the rifle twelve times,
felt the recoil of air against
my knobby shoulder. I
saw the fear still stuck
on its tiny face. I
felt the twitch
of luck leaving its pressed
fur as its hind foot
kicked its last kick.

No one spoke.
I heard the whir of bicycle
wheels when I bent to feel
its still-perked ears.

I tossed the limp body
in the soybean field behind my house,
each stalk crisp from an overfeeding sun.
I whispered the closest thing
I knew to a prayer: *I'm sorry.*
Its body snapped a circle
into the field where Mom
couldn't see, the sun winking pink
behind the cottonwood trees.

Fishing Stories

The drive is almost as good as the fishing.
The pavement is smooth from Kansas to Missouri,
then gravel crunches a rugged tune with our tires.
We listen to oldies: Journey,
Guns 'N Roses, Motley Crue.
We resist the urge to sing along.
No matter how good the song,
Dad says dudes don't sing in the car
with other dudes.
Humming falls under gray area.
We tap our feet in time instead.

The leftover night sky lightens into orange
in the east and we drive into its glow.
Our boat follows us down the road, hitched
to our every sway between highway lines.

Mostly we're quiet.
We breathe, shift, sip black coffee.
Every so often, between songs
and our tapping feet, when a sound
or light reflecting off the truck's hood
catches him just right,
Dad speaks.

As we near the lake, he tells fishing stories
the way fishermen do.
But these are true.
The words filling the cab of our truck
glimpse into his past
like a paintbrush into a bucket.
The stories make me yearn for water
beneath our boat, bass and crappie and bluegill
searching for our fiery lures.
The stories usually go
a little something like this...

Green Acre 3

Big Fish Territory

The swollen stars spoke
to one another in bright whispers
above our boat so the planets
wouldn't hear.

Dad's breath rose and joined
mine in wind that stole it,
wind cold as water
churning at the bottom of the lake.

The green-tipped tail
of a shooting star falling toward
Earth, yearning to touch
rich Kansas soil, bloomed
bright, and I pointed.

We smiled, still hushed
by the planets when my pole
bent half-over and our boat
nearly tipped into the shining
image of stars
bouncing on water.

The belly of our boat thrashed
against the blurred reflection
of stars on waves.
Bait jumped and splashed
in the sliding bucket.

Our boat, everything in it,
converged to meet
the pale-finned body
rising from the furious lake.

The Death of Santa

My brother and I would run
from our bedrooms in synchronous
at 2 a.m., unable to sleep on Christmas
Eve, to see what Santa brought.

Gifts from our parents
lay in the shadows under
our red-blue-green-lit Christmas tree.
But Santa's gifts sat stacked
in front, glowing in the twinkled
light bursts, wrapping paper
seeming to pulse.
We sat cross-legged on the carpet,
not touching, just looking.
We'd sit for hours, staring, waiting
to run and wake Mom up.

We never questioned
the handwritten tags that looked
just like Mom's curled cursive.
Or the light-slicked shine of paper
that matched the gifts piled
under the tree.

In the young, cold hours of Christmas
morning, for years, we checked the plate
of peanut butter cookies Mom made,
crumbs carefully left,
celery stalks half-chewed,
what Mom and Dad didn't eat
cooling in the fridge.

One year Santa didn't show.
Those shine-wrapped boxes ceased.
My brother and I knew.
We knew, and our parents knew,
the house and the tree knew,
the handwritten nametags knew,
the uncooked cookies and the snow
beginning to fall outside knew,
all without anyone saying a word.

Mending Time

When my grandparents' house burned,
left hollow like a cicada's shell,
they waited ten years to rebuild it.

The barren kitchen still echoes
with scents of holidays and reunion,
home-cooked aromas embedded
in brick the flames couldn't quite lick off.

Fiberglass threads hanging in the blank air
shimmer like my grandma's hoop earrings,
melted and lost.

I remember where the refrigerator once stood,
every inch covered in blurry pictures
and my crayon-slick papers.

We always watched hummingbirds
slurp sugar-water from the feeder,
shooting long tongues like lily petals.
That window is empty now,
glass tempered and broken on the ground.

The house is coming back from the dead,
heartbeat sparked and irregular.
The musty pheromones of fresh wood
and insulation swell in the air,
accents of sheet rock and nails close behind.

Memories baked into the foundation
like happy scars, churning scents
of browned rolls and chocolate turtles
while the house inhales, sipping in new air.

The First Dog I Ever Knew

My grandpa hit Pup with his rusted
Ford pickup, backing out
of the driveway one Sunday
when I was twelve.

I ran outside and slid under the truck,
tears threatening to spill over.
Pup lay there beneath the rusted chunks
of metal, his curling fur a matted mess,
ratted from wading in the pond that day.
His muzzle turned to me, white with age.
His eyes opened wide, pleading.

Gravel dug at my side.
Pup's eyes went blank,
still open, empty, staring into me.

I saw Pup's eyes—as pocks on the moon,
pinpricks of stars, shadows hugging
indents on my bedroom ceiling,
the headlights of highlighted school busses,
the empty sockets in Grandpa's head—
for months after.

I-70 to St. Louis

Dirty cocksucker, Dad groaned alongside the backing tenor vocals of his car horn. My brother and I knew *dirty cocksucker* was bad. That exact combination of words, dirty, cock, sucker, drew the attention of the universe to our car like beaming spotlights on escaped convicts. We were a neon blip on the radar of the All-Knowing. Dalton and I silently snickered, waiting for more. Mom rested her head against her window's cool glass, a blonde mannequin, hair speckled with the gray my brother and I never dared mention. Dad waved his middle finger around with each pump of the brakes.

Car after *cocksucker* car we passed. Drivers offered a slew of obscene gestures that Dad gladly returned. Toyotas painted in *cocksucker* greens and blacks cut Dad off; *cocksucker* semis inched along in the fast lane. Mom glared back at us, shaking her head, and finally laughed. And then, as all our laughter permeated the car, Dad chuckled too. We were now a vague, hazy cocksucker blip disappearing over the cocksucker horizon of the dirty cocksucker highway.

Dam

I drove my car down the Sugar Valley Lake dam junior year of high school. I wasn't drunk on liquor or beer, no drugs in my system. I was drunk with the beauty of the night and the comradery of my friends who would become strangers a decade later. But that night we were young and fast and invincible and close as brothers.

We rode my piece of shit cavalier down the steep decline like a thoroughbred to fetch tires we'd rolled down. Our laughter split the night, and we didn't care. The trees were dark steeples against the gaping moon and they bowed to us. My car's tiny engine whined during the descent, but we didn't hear it—blood pumped louder in our ears. When we hit the ditch at the bottom, we stopped laughing.

My friends said something like *ah, shit, dude* and left to get help, but I was stranded there, high-centered in a ditch, radiator hissing steam, nothing but the night and my dead iPod to comfort me. All those trees laughed, crisp leaves cackling like hyenas in the wind.

Catfishing the Elk City Reservoir, ft. Bugs

Midnight. Our boat rocks, double-anchored
in a river connected to the lake,
one of a curving mass of slivers snaking to the
      reservoir, fingers
running back to the den of fish and big, black water.

We sit in a swarming mass of insect buzz,
crashing wings and abdomens
against the blazoned light of our lanterns.
Insect feet on our naked faces, arms, necks, force
into our dirty clothes like the water
surging past our lines and hooks.

I pull my shirt up over my face, to breathe, to cough,
to avoid a mouthful of the dense fog of bugs.

Mosquitos, craneflies, June bugs, gnats, dobsonflies
grown from hellgrammites, giant mayflies,
      moths and dragonflies—
all come to devour the heat and light, primal.

All night we catch nothing but useless dinosaur-scaled
      gar
who steal our baited bluegill and swim around us,
sharp-toothed as sharks, long-sleek-gray torpedoes,
glaring glow-eyed from just under the empty water,
      winking.

Even after we dim the lanterns to lessen the swarm,
more bugs seek us out. The life of the river and trees
has already been disturbed—nature sends these bugs
like white blood cells to take us out.

Pests

after Victoria Chang

Pests—Died my whole life as needed.
I was taught to kill all pests plaguing
our house. Glue traps. Poison. Raid.
Flat-headed shovel   for black snakes.
Mom squealing *kill it!* but would never
dirty her hands   with the killing.
Secondhand guilt is less viscous, water
off the backs of house sparrows.
Death was default   punishment for
intrusion, inconvenience. Pinprick
pain, quick, boot   stomped, fly
swatter cocked, breath   silenced.
I imagine the collective souls hover
the grounds   of that green acre,
a shimmering gas,   pink and blue
luminescence when struck by sunlight,
waiting to descend   on intruders,
cricket song, mouse   squeal, garter hiss
houseflyhoneybeemuddobberyellowjacket
buzz cascading all around.

50 Words for Nostalgia

After "50 Words for Nostalgia" by Daniel Miller

the plastic-strummed guitar hero notes / the glass clank of jones soda / the sweaty room / the midnight dark / mom spraying febreeze / little brother watching / the rush of crushing riffs / the rush of friday night / the rush of nowhere else to be / the hush of pals / rushing to forget each other

So Many Towns Away

The Kansas night sky feels like home.
Those stars soften the empty black
and comfort me, so many towns away
from home where I imagine
Mom is thinking about me.

Mom sits on the front porch, swinging
in the glider, one foot dangles.
She puffs a cigarette, tip blazing
like her chipped nail polish,
sends swirls of smoke upward
into the nothing that joins the stars.

The wind blows, the streetlight flickers
on and off and back on again.
A chained mutt down the street barks,
rusted metal clacks barely audible.
Mom is unfazed.
She's waited all day to live this moment,
nothing left to distract her thinking.

Both her boys off to college now,
so many towns away.
The house holds less breath, so she's turned
our bedroom lights on.
She's scattered the house with the clothes
we left behind, to trick herself.
She's sat in both our beds to fill the cold
blankets with some kind of warmth.
She's checked all the channels on TV,
but nothing's on.

Now she finishes her last cigarette.
Sips the last sips of her sweetened coffee.
Under the stars, calm, her breathing
is slow, deliberate.

Inside the phone rings.
She flicks her cigarette into the dampening grass,
grabs her slick mug, and hops inside
to find my name on the caller I.D.

Chrysalism in November

Rain patters against earth
outside my window, whispers
a song back to Kansas
cumulonimbus clouds.

The sloped ditch by Pine Street
runs a soft brown like mint-
sprinkled cocoa. My breath
gathers on the thin pane.

Lightning flashes first, smooth,
golden like waking
from a good, good dream.
Then the warm blanketing
of thunder above somewhere,
everywhere, like Zeus
reminding the Midwest
He is still here.

6'4" 300 lb Male Walks Home at Night

The moon hangs low in the sky,
dropping light through tree limbs
on my walk home from campus.
October, black Batman hoodie,
backpack hanging from shoulders.

Kylee might have dinner ready—
she does that sometimes
when I'll get home late.
The dogs will jump on me, go crazy.

The shortcut from Grubbs Hall
to my duplex, a loose path
of scattered gravel, winds between
a house and the campus ministry.

Sudden footsteps in front of me
jerk my head up, choke away
breath caught in my diaphragm.
Nobody else around to yell for.

A woman, jeans, purple jacket,
walks my direction, sees me, stops,
phone screen showing wide eyes,
lips splitting apart like a fault,
turns back the way she came, fast.

I reach the mouth of the path
where the buildings stop. She's gone.
Her shadow has slipped, spilled
around the building, sprinted away from me.

I lean against a tree, take a breath,
feel the grainy bark.
I think to apologize, yell out
into the darkness, soften her fear,
but she's gone, a held breath dispersed.
My heart still beats fast, hard,
panicked against my ribcage.

Catching a 65-Pound Blue Catfish

Dad and I sat out in the middle of a lake by the power plant with two poles each in the water and we'd just lit the orange glow of our only cigars at three a.m. when one of my poles bent half-over and damn-near popped out of its rod-holder. "Holy shit!" I yelled. Dad started reeling the other poles like crazy, lines sounding like wind slicing through tree limbs, so we wouldn't get a knotted cluster-fuck under our boat. I got ahold of my live pole and reared back to set the hook and let out a big groan around my cigar and Dad kept on reeling while our aluminum boat started to turn and get pulled by that big goddamn fish.

"Shit, it's big," I yelled and tried to reel in some line but that catfish was strong and kept pulling out my drag. A cranking squeal echoed through the open Kansas air draped over us. Dad went to grab my other pole and knocked our only propane lantern into the lake and he yelled out as all the light went away and I kept on reeling in the early morning black.

We flipped our headlamps on and for the next fifteen minutes we existed as two small blips of light on that big black lake under the bigger, star-pocked Kansas sky. I made some headway reeling in line as the fish swam toward me. The tip of my pole was still bent over double, pointing like an arrow to where the fish swam, frantic. It finally breached the surface, a foaming splash before dragging more of my line back down. "Let the fucker tire itself out," Dad said, "stop horsing it."
So, I stopped horsing it and let the fish swim and pull in a frothing circle.

Finally, I got it close enough to the boat that Dad could reach it. "Too big for the net," he said, and put on a pair of gloves to grab it by the jaw. He managed to get a tight grip and pull that bastard out of the water, groaning a man's groan I was sure I'd never groaned before, the fish splashing in a fit of panic.

Its white belly lay flush with the hollowed bottom of our
        boat,
eyes glowing red in our headlamp light,
all of us dead tired, adrenaline racing,
everything else dark as the Kansas sky
since Dad knocked our lantern in the lake.

We looked at it, not speaking.
Just watching, breathing, both smiling.
"Nice job, buddy," Dad said.
We pounded clenched fists
the way guys do. We fished on
until daylight, nothing more to catch.
Nothing else we needed to catch.
Dad caught nothing, but that blue fish,
a fighter, a hell of fun to bring in,
now tied off in the water beside us,
was enough.

The propane from our lantern bubbled up for hours,
until the sun rose and cauterized
the clouds off in the west while that pale fish
swam and pushed its mass
against the belly of our boat,
bumping, bumping, bumping
in the stained-glass morning.

Certainty

I.
We first met at a golf course.
Hole eight, midnight.
Our friends, the other couple,
disappeared at hole nine.
I remember we walked all three pars
holding hands, our hips bumping,
stars dropping light on watered turf.

We kissed for no good reason.
I'd first seen your face
not three hours before, in the dark,
but we sat there, moon fizzling
through limbs, dew gathering on us,
so what the hell?

II.
October morning chill. Sun still pink
under the warm horizon. The sky blank,
except for Jupiter and Venus, glowing hot.
The dogs pee, sniff,
knowing my wife has filled
their food bowls. They're certain.
In what world would their food
not be waiting inside after morning potty?

She kisses me quickly, leaves
for work. I watch her drive away
past all the shining dew.

Nowhere Sunday

The wind flicks our boat around the lake
like smoothed pucks on a shuffleboard.
Dad puts me in charge of navigation.
Which means I dick with the trolling motor
and cuss openly every so often.

Grandpa's line breaks. Breaks again.
Each time, my little brother must pause
his fishing, use his young vision to see
the line through each narrowing eye
and tie Grampa's jig with Palomar knots.

Back home, I'm busy, behind, essays
stacked, flower beds weed-infested.
The front steps of my house
crumble, concrete disintegrating
like Styrofoam in gasoline.

But out here, grandpa snores. Dad reels
in the biggest fish of the day. Sun
warms skin, tobacco buzzes lips. Dalton
and I recite movie quotes, annoy Dad,
like we're back in elementary school,

and that's all we ever had.

Back Home

I.
My dad tells me
how we played catch
when I was younger.
Here's my glove, he says,
patting the cracked leather,
rubbing the old creases.
It creaks like tree limbs
as he struggles
to squeeze his hand
back inside.

II.
In the northeast corner
of my old bedroom
where the doorframe meets
the cobwebbed corner,
that one-inch gap of space
is still crayon slick where
blue and green and angry red
got back at mom and Dad.
They must've taken a toy
or turned off Batman
or made me or come back
inside before darkness fell.

III.
My wife narrows her eyes
when I call my hometown,
Pleasanton, *Home*. She says,
home is with me. With us. *Our* house.
The highway hums against our tires
as we drive there. The wind sighs by.
I compromise.
Back home, I say. Back home
where my brother and I adventured
in the furious snow each winter,
where we reeled in tons of fish
with Dad and Grandpa,
where my family all sat bundled
with coffee to watch the Chiefs and Jayhawks,
where Mom, crying, handed me my diploma,
where the sun's sure, burning magenta
faded over the Haines house to close the day,
where I grew into myself.
Back home, I say.
We're headed back home.

The Sound of Casting a Fishing Pole

A deep, radiant dream—
the whizz of line flung, crack
and splash of hook and bait,
a harmony out of the black,
at once heard but forgotten as quickly.

And minutes later, heard again,
the furious uncranking of line
to be reeled taut, then reeled in 30 minutes later
with a twisting squeal that changes
from howl to echo
as the scaled shine of bait skis the surface—

all to be forgotten,
mind struggling to remember
while lying in bed, slipping to sleep,
head padded by pillows,
until a month later fishing again.

How many sounds are like that—
my mother's hysterical laugh,
an arrow loosed from tensed bowstring,
my corgi's howl that chases sirens,
the sputtering exhaust of my grandpa's old Ford,
the metallic crash of weights against a squat rack,
my aunt's old Kodak that popped with each shutter
        flash—
special sounds, heard and forgotten,
taken for granted by the mind
until you can't even hear
their echoes
in your head?

Chiropractic

Pain
takes hold again,
pervasive, Virginia winter creeper
climbing up, vines growing outward in winding green
  buds,
tendrils spreading across surface, wind through cracks,
  sappy adhesive with
its oxalate crystals that burn skin, beautiful blue berries
  oxalic-acid-toxic, difficult to maintain
or remove, all stemming from that innocent bulb
  planted in fertile soil, ripe for something
  painful to take hold.

Losing Batman

My old bedroom
in my parents' house
is ridden with fine dust
in the dark.
All four corners
softened by nests
of threaded cobweb.

Movie posters hang
on every inch of wall
to cover the ugly
flower wallpaper.
Dozens of thumbtacks
hold them in time.

Through the dust and dark
I see Captain America,
Transformers, 300.
Further back, Harry Potter
looms in high school—
posters, my comforter,
a cardboard cutout.

Even fainter is the Batman
theme once layering my room.
Posters, pencil drawings
colored within the lines.
Mint-condition action figures.
The massive black kite
thumbtacked to the ceiling
over my bed.

I grew too old
for the caped crusader,
too cool
for the boy who lived.

Now, in my old room,
I won't look under my bed.
What if I find
my seven-year-old self
hiding there, tears shining
his pudgy face,
devastated I would take
Batman from the only room
in the house
he could call his own.

The Losses of Maxine Johnson

Lying there on display, the whole town gathered to honor a lost information hub, my grandmother looks at rest, but isn't. Her body has morphed—inactivity, dementia, Alzheimer's, mouth having lost words, the yarns she'd spun; muscle having lost memory, how to jump rope, how to finely thread yarn between yarn; mind having lost everything else.

Her dentures had to be buried with her. My aunt obsessed over taking them, to fit into her own tooth-decayed mouth. She was absent at the end, during the hardest six years, a reversal of the typical, and yet was owed Grandma's teeth. *It's the least you can give me.* At the end, just as the middle and beginning, Grandma was expected to give everything. My mother, though, saved her that final possession.

Once, my wife and I visited her, the assisted living building looming like the overcast day. Inside, we tried to communicate. We told her about an upcoming trip, our recent anniversary. Kylee complimented her purple sequined jacket. I exclaimed how goddamn good the Chiefs and Patrick Mahomes are. Her eyes widened at "Chiefs," electricity opening in the darkened room of her KC sports fandom. She laughed so hard, so loud, a nurse ran to check on us. Tears shined in three sets of eyes, laughing our asses off. This is my last memory of Grandma: hysterics, her real self sparkling through like the blinding corona of an eclipse.

At the service, the local pastor speaks of Grandma's faith, which she'd never had. He tells the town he'd asked her three days prior if she accepted Christ as her lord, wanted to be saved, and she'd nodded *yes*. Maybe she knew what he was asking. I dare not deny her that. But to presume communication with the woman who was no longer my grandmother, rewrite her history to the town, was to walk over, rip the dentures from her mouth.

Counting Hawks

I count hawks perched
on the roadside as I drive.
The highway pavement whirrs
like an open country wind
beneath my car.

I remember gravel grinding under
my grandpa's Ford pickup
when he took me to cut wood.

We always wore coats and gloves,
blue jeans, long johns
pressing warmth against our skin.

As we drove, Ford groaning in the cold,
we counted hawks on power lines,
on fence posts, tree branches.
Grandpa called them chicken hawks.

Whoever counts the most wins, Grandpa's words
floated beneath his thick mustache, churning in a fog
that filled the cab like ghosts and I looked to count.

I'd forget the December
morning cold, the wood needing cut,
so early the sun hadn't cracked the skyline
and my cartoons only existed in the TV guide.

An Apologia for This Pint of Boulevard Unfiltered Wheat

The stars outside drink in
the Friday night and this Kansas
winter-cold glass—frothing
with dense foam that just kisses
both lemon wedges—
sweats like lovers down
to the waxed table and coaster and
the dim bar lights filter through ale that
glows like time-frozen sap to amber,
bronzed mosquitos caught mid-buzz.
Citrus and hops drift
behind the music,
up to my thirsty face,
and why the hell not?

Storm, a Pantoum

A storm is thickening off in the west,
the neon glow of lightning faint behind
the lurid party of clouds tumbling in.
We sit in my truck, sheltered from the coming rain.

The neon glow of lightning is faint behind
the wild woods surrounding the abandoned farm,
so we sit in my truck, sheltered from the coming rain.
Wind gusts cascade down a volley of leaves.

The wild woods surrounding the abandoned farm
seem to sway as one body, each tree moving in unison.
Wind gusts cascade down a volley of leaves
as our breath grows thick on each pane of glass.

We sway as one body, both of us moving in unison.
Light rain pings on the hood of my truck
as our breath grows thick on each pane of glass
and everything is varnished in condensation.

Light rain pings on the hood of my truck,
the lurid party of clouds still tumbling in.
Everything is varnished in condensation
as the storm thickens off in the west.

Sweat and Marijuana

My grandma, speaking of
meeting my grandpa
for the first time in 1969

He was high with his brother and friends
that night—their corner of the bowling alley
reeked of grass.
The lights above their lane flicked
like lightning cracks in storms back home,
blurring the scuffed shapes of pins
ready to be knocked down
in a popping crash of thunder.

Led Zeppelin's "Good Times, Bad Times"
hung in the air between us like smoke.
I leaned my shoulder blades against the bar,
cold can of Schlitz in hand, drinking
all of him in.

He sat on a black and white-cushioned bench,
legs skinny and lax as boiled linguini
with toned arms that propped up his scrawny,
war-shaken body.
He was sweating down from his thick,
black hair, just showing on clean-shaven skin
as the lights flicked again.

Cigarette smoke poured over me as I drank my beer,
but I imagined he smelled like sweat and oil,
that man-sweat that smells good.

They all laughed about nothing.
His laugh was the loudest, the hardest,
sound coming out as a wheeze at the end.
He looked over at me and my friend on barstools,
cutting the laughter if only for a second,
my look stripping the hysterics from him.
His smile thinned, teeth just showing,
like he still does now if I look quick enough.

I finished my beer and imagined his smell again,
that smell of sweat and marijuana I knew
I wanted smothered into my skin that night.

Fishing in Illinois by
Uncle Rodge's Cabin

The lake wakes before us, sits there,
early fog morning, eats leaves and tadpoles
to shake away sleep while the sun blooms.

Drink black coffee, Dad and Rodge talk
about rainfall, who's had luck fishing lately.
Dalton readies the boat, rods propped,
motor mounted, hooks sharp.

Cool. Sun barely winks up, we throw
our first casts, lines whirl through air,
lake swallows. Hooked plastic bait—
theirs purple worms, mine pumpkin seed craw.
        No bites. No noise.

Our boat a ghost, moves
us corner to corner, passes dead corn fields,
acres and acres all around.
We work our rods, jig, reel slow,
line spools back up, spits mist
of lake water in the boat.

Rodge sits by the cabin, puffs cigar, yells over the water,
the sunken island, all the trees reaching up
like fingers,
        "goddamn, you guys gonna catch anything or
what?"
Echo rings out, as if from miles off, follows the dam,
dies in the lake somewhere by North cove.
We don't say anything, smile, just cast again.

We catch four fish. Just four,
all bass, largemouth, all thrown back.
Breakfast cooks as we dock,
bacon and egg sizzle thrown our way,
Aunt Bobbie cooks, Mom helps,
Rodge still puffs, denim jeans, jacket.
Older than I remember.

But there's that lake. Been fishing there
two decades, Dad two decades before that.
It'll be there, big, moss-edged, fish-full,
boat docked, sacred, decades more.
Decades away,

                                        free of time.

About the Poet

Cody Shrum is a two-time Pushcart Prize-nominated Kansas writer and editor. He received his BA and MA degrees in creative writing from Pittsburg State University, and his MFA in creative writing and media arts from The University of Missouri-Kansas City. His writing has appeared in such publications as *HAD*, *Major 7th Magazine*, *BULL*, *Cleaver Magazine*, *The Midwest Quarterly*, *Rust + Moth*, and *Harbor Review*, as well as the anthology, *Kansas Time + Place: An Anthology of Heartland Poetry*. He is also a fiction editor for *Identity Theory*. Cody's writing explores the rural Midwest and, more specifically, small-town Kansas where he grew up. As the cover of this chapbook attests, he has always been a huge nerd and Batman fan. Cody lives in Kansas City with his wife, Kylee, and their two ferocious guard dogs, Zeus and Phoebe.

Credits

These poems have appeared or are forthcoming in the following publications, some in altered form:

Bear Review: "Nowhere Sunday"

Harbor Review: "I-70 to St. Louis"
      *Nominated for a Pushcart prize.

Heartland: Poems of Love, Resistance, and Solidarity: "Certainty" and "So Many Towns Away"

Johnson County Library Staff Picks Blog: "Catfishing the Elk City Reservoir, ft. Bugs"
      *Won The Reluctant I Writing Contest

Kansas Time + Place: "An Apologia for this Pint of Boulevard Unfiltered Wheat" "Big Fish Territory" "Mending Time"

Major 7th Magazine: "Sweat and Marijuana"

Rust + Moth: "First Date at Dr. Plumm's"

The Coop: A Poetry Cooperative: "6'4" 300 lb Male Walks Home at Night"

The Midwest Quarterly: "Pests"

Acknowledgements

Many thanks to Laura Lee Washburn, Chris Anderson, Lori Martin, and my entire Pittsburg State poetry workshop family, without whom none of these poems would exist and I wouldn't be a poet or writer in the first place.

Though I only took one poetry course at UMKC, thanks also to Hadara Bar-Nadav and my cohort of fellow students for workshopping some of these poems during that crazy COVID lockdown semester.

And of course, a million thanks to my loving family, who have always supported and championed my writing. In many ways this collection is a snapshot of, and a love letter to, all of you.

I was lucky enough to snag some killer blurbs from a few amazing writers who are way out of my league. Thanks to Melissa Fite Johnson, Allison Blevins, Aaron Burch, and David Lee. I will be forever grateful both for your kind words and for reading this book without much notice when you didn't have to.

Thanks, also, to the journals and editors who published some of these poems previously.

Lastly, thanks to *Choeofpleirn Press* and the 2024 Jonathan Holden Chapbook Contest judge, Steve Brisendine, for selecting my manuscript as the top finalist.

Jonathan Holden Poetry

Chapbook Contest

First Time Poets

Submit your poetry chapbooks of 25-40 pages

By April 30, 2025

$20 entry fee

Winning poet receives $250, 10 copies of the print book, and free social media advertising

Follow our Submission Guidelines:

https://www.choeofpleirnpress.com/poetry-chapbook-contest

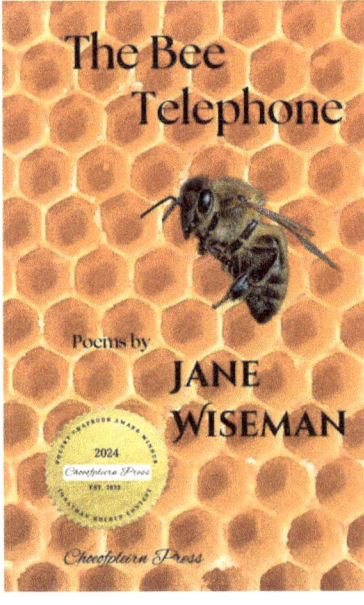

2024 Winner
Jonathan Holden Poetry
Chapbook Contest

Hosted by
Choeofpleirn Press

Imagine picking up a phone and hearing an alien voice or pressing our noses against glass to watch aliens work.

Jane Wiseman allows us to tune in to the sights and sounds of our universe, even though they may seem as alien as listening to *The Bee Telephone*.

Green Acre 42

2nd Finalist

Jonathan Holden Poetry
Chapbook Contest
2024

How do we shake the detritus from our memories? A geographic transplant, Rochelle Germond washes clean those memories she rediscovers before leaving those excavations behind to discover not only what can frighten her but also what gives meaning to this new location where "the wishbone we snap breaks evenly in half, / a sure sign that we will both receive our pleas."

James P. Cooper

Author of *Listening for Low Tide*
Honorable Mention for the Eric
Hoffer Book Award

Available at Amazon and
Choeofpleirn Press

Listening for Low Tide

Too much happens at ground level:
the kids selling candy or delivering
newspapers shortcut through the yard,
the neighbors' dogs blare their alarms
in unison, and teens, shielded by the heartbeat
of their music, speed down the street.

Two stories above the ground,
I welcome the afternoon sunlight
as it stretches across the rug,
my cat moving with it. From the opposite
window, the shadows cast by trees
overspread the ground, the sunlight only
hitting the treetops. Sound waves lap
against the building, the tide at its lowest
each night when the owl in the park
starts to hoot its presence.

Choeofpleirn Press
www.choeofpleirnpress.com
2024

Green Acre 44